Introduction:

Mom has Alzheimer's
What do we do now?

Hi, I'm Ron Schaeffer, author of nine published books and three not yet published. I am also a caregiver to my lovely mother-in-law, Miss Betty, an Alzheimer's patient. Throughout this book I will refer to her as, mom.

After doing considerable research on the subject of Alzheimer's and working with mom for over five years, I decided I would write this small book for individuals who find themselves faced with the challenges of this dreaded disease.

There is little research available to the public concerning this killer and hopefully, this book will help the caregiver and the families of individuals dying from this malady in their understanding of what their loved one suffers and what can be done to make them comfortable.

Many people take on the responsibility of caregiver without any real knowledge of what this disease is and what happens to the Alzheimer patient as he or she progresses through the stages. We also do not recognize the disease until it has developed in our loved one for as many as two years.

It is only natural we wish to care for our loved ones no matter what care is required and the care required for an Alzheimer's patient is little different from the care we might give a child with cancer or some

other malady. The problem with Alzheimer's is the debilitating effects of the illness, as it lingers on year after year, becoming most unbearable for the patient and the caregiver.

Hopefully, this book will assist the caregivers in understanding those challenges ahead. I can attest that this disease should not be taken lightly. It is the most devastating disease I have ever encountered in my 76 years.

I offer my heart and my prayers to all of you who take on the responsibility of caregiver and all my love to your patients. I wish nothing but the best for your health and the health of your loved one as you struggle to understand this terrible disease.

I hope this little book will help you understand what it is you are working with so you can better deal with the outcome.

Ron

Dedication:

I would like to dedicate this book to my wonderful Mother-in-law who taught me the value of patience required to work with an individual suffering from this horrendous, debilitating disease. I would also like to thank my wonderful wife for assisting me in this task and standing by my decision to take care of her mother.

This has been a challenging, heartbreaking decision on my part and the part of the family as they watch their mother suffer from the most debilitating disease in our century.

I would like to also commend any individual who takes on the responsibility of caring for their loved one suffering from this disease and offer you my prayers.

Just remember, your Alzheimer sufferer deserves every bit of your love and your support.

Ron

Mom Has Alzheimer's
What do we do now?

Caring for your loved one with Alzheimer's

By

Ron Schaeffer

Mom Has Alzheimer's

What do we do now?

Caring for your loved one with Alzheimer's

ISBN: 978-1-300-50204-3

For information Address Contact:

Ron

@

www.ronaldeschaeffer.com

Chapter One

Alzheimer's What is it?

I suppose it is imperative I expound my thoughts about those diseases plaguing our world and blame industrial growth for all the maladies manifesting themselves into our society but that would be an unfair attack on industrialization.

There are a number of different schools of thought about Alzheimer's and those different ideas can be confusing to the layperson. Some individuals give the disease three stages while others say there are five; some believe six and others believe there are seven distinct stages. There are those who believe industrial pollution causes the disease and others who believe it is genetic.

For the purpose of this book, since I see a tremendous amount of overlapping of symptoms I tend toward the idea that it is just one crappy disease that lingers on for many years and then eventually kills the patient. I will therefore adopt the idea of seven stages and deal with each stage as individually as possible.

As for the industrialization theory, well, the disease has been around for over one hundred years, so the idea of food borne disease might be out of the question. Then again, there is always that possibility that industrialization has some bearing on mental deterioration of the individual. I prefer to leave that question open.

As a caregiver to my mother-in-law who has Alzheimer's I am particularly concerned with how this disease came to run amuck in our society for the last

100 years and not one scientist or one researcher has come up with a cure. They were able to cure AIDS within a few years but that was because it started creeping into the society of the rich and famous. I have no doubt that AIDS would still be a threat if it only affected the poor and when you think about it, only the rich can afford the medicines available.

I am not convinced Alzheimer's is a disease of our own stupidity, our greed and our lust for the better life. I know the disease has been with us for over one hundred years and therefore is probably genetic in nature and not produced environmentally. I am however, of the opinion that chemicals used by our companies and demanded by our government along with certain gene defects caused by our environment and perhaps gene mutations are the chief causes of many diseases introduced into our bodies through our water supplies, food supplies and especially drugs from our drug companies. I have a particular aversion toward Fluorides, Mercury and food additives used for preserving our perishable products. Diseases like Alzheimer's and Autism could very easily be more pronounced in our present day society from those particular chemicals.

Although Alzheimer's is simply called Dementia it is much more complicated than that. Dementia is a simple way of shrugging off a disease that causes considerably more pain and suffering than forgetfulness. Alzheimer's is a killer of not just the old but also anyone who comes down with it. This is not just an old age disease; it attacks the young and the old.

Beliefs years ago labeled people with Dementia simply crazy; the society categorized those individuals who were different from the so-called norm into one category and threw them all into some institution. It was a simple solution to a complex problem and an easy

way of dealing with the unwanted members of the society who did not fit the mores of so-called normal. It is easy understanding the idea of, out of sight so out of mind. If you throw them all into some dungeon you do not have to worry or think about them.

Today we have a more humane approach to mental illnesses and mental disorders but we still have hundreds of thousands of individuals living on the streets suffering from one disorder or another.

No one took the time or made any effort to actually attempt diagnosing individuals suffering from forgetfulness to see if there were differences in symptoms from the many people institutionalized and deemed crazy. Nor did anyone take the time or make the effort to see if everyone in a mental institution suffering from memory loss could possibly suffer from some medical malady. Even in the fifties we still threw our relatives into a mental institution when they showed signs of severe dementia.

The labels, crazy, stupid or possessed covered a great deal of ground and labeling all these people together made the diagnosis simple. It also meant the so-called normal people would shun them for fear of being contaminated. I imagine there were other beliefs that stigmatized the afflicted.

I would not openly blame my government for bringing about diseases but I doubt they are interested in any sort of cure and I doubt they really care what we citizens think.

Our government has become the very monster we didn't want when this country originated. I believe our government has become callous to the needs of the people in such a way that the quest for more government power debilitates the quest for better living conditions and better, longer life for the individual. In plain words, it is more convenient to euthanize the old,

the young, and ignore the invalid than find ways to make them comfortable in their surroundings by alleviating their pain and suffering or eliminating the root causes of our diseases in the first place.

After all, it is my understanding that most of our politicians interpret the meaning of health care as a euphemism for euthanasia. It appears our government finds it too costly and too difficult to care for the old or the handicapped.

That said, I believe the chemicals we produce and then cram into our food supply coupled with the massive pollution we create, including the fluorides in our water supply, not to mention the mercury poisoning going on that our government refuses to acknowledge, are most of the reasons we see increases in diseases like Alzheimer's, Autism, and other debilitating infirmities.

I have never been much on conspiracy theories but when diseases like AIDS, suddenly pop up out of the clear blue supposedly originating in some specie of monkey and then somehow mutating into the human world, I find those explanations difficult to believe and impossible to accept.

If you think about AIDS, when it emerged from Africa, there was no cure and no immediate remedies; it was and probably still is the perfect virus. I am sorry but I cannot help but be suspicious of our government or our drug companies in many of these cases, especially when the general history of our politicians is suspect at best. I remember the many experiments our government did in the name of science on our military personnel, especially those Americans serving in the military who were black. There is no excuse for the degradation suffered by the blacks in our military by the hands of our government.

I believe it is time the American people stand their ground and made a few demands regarding the chemicals crammed into our food supply or our drugs.

I do not believe these new diseases are the result of too much carbon in our atmosphere; I believe they are being manufactured through our desire to make things safer. We have a desire to live longer but we are sacrificing the quality of life for the quantity of life.

What good is it to live twenty years longer if eighteen of those years are lived in pain, suffering or loss of memory? Alzheimer's is a disease that totally destroys the memory and the body. It is a terrible disease and a terrible death sentence.

The Elderly

I remember taking care of my grandfather just before he died and I remember his senility. He had difficulty remembering things but his brain did not shut down completely; on occasion, he could still feed himself and recall people and particulars from the past. His short-term memory was sluggish but it still worked. In fact, I do not remember any disease with symptoms like Alzheimer's from my youth.

I am told from my research that the disease was here long before a hundred years ago but I guess those individuals suffering from it were removed from society and hidden from public view. I visited the institute for the insane at Salem, Oregon on two occasions gathering information for a book I wrote. I believe I had contact with a few individuals with Alzheimer's on those occasions but back then the disease had a different label.

Those individuals afflicted with the disease were there at the mental institution but in Oregon, back then, they were labeled insane. I do believe history records

those with the disease as being mentally unbalanced and I believe my visits proved that to be true. That would explain why the disease did not come to the forefront of society until someone actually identified it as an ailment not associated with a mental disorder. Even after it was identified, states like Oregon still kept those afflicted in mental institutions.

When I was younger, I spent considerable time in nursing homes entertaining the guests; I played the piano for their comfort and enjoyment. I even engaged in a few chess games with those who needed someone new to slaughter. I discovered quickly that old men who play chess are a lot smarter than me.

None of those elderly gentlemen or ladies showed symptoms like the symptoms associated with Alzheimer's, so, it makes sense that relatives with the disease were institutionalized for the sake of the families embarrassment.

I realize there is no public outcry about this disease but I believe there should be. Even if the disease is genetical and not environmentally caused we should demand from our government to quit wasting money on food stamps and get to work on research that would end diseases like Autism and Alzheimer's. We should demand from our government more research into the cause of this disease and possibly a cure or an abatement of the symptoms. These diseases need not exist; they can be eliminated.

If you spend any time at all with an Alzheimer patient, you will begin believing as I do. We must find cures for this and other diseases, many of which are man-made.

Currently, there are studies concerning these considerations and our hope is someone will come up with a study that actually makes sense and finds cures for Autism and Alzheimer's. I believe those cures are

forthcoming and I believe they are in the near future but will they be implemented considering the impact on the preservative industry or the impact on the medical industry?

We must conclude that the power of the chemical industry is greater than the power of the people. When the people finally get the idea that many of these diseases come from industrial poisons, they might stand their ground and demand answers. Until that time our loved ones will have to suffer and die from these dreaded diseases.

Chapter Two
The Role of the Caregiver

Taking care of an Alzheimer patient is a full time, 24 hour a day job. Before we get into the facts of this disease it is important for you as a caregiver to understand that this is a real disease; it has been around for a long time even though we did not begin understanding it until just a few years ago.

Individuals with loved ones showing symptoms of this disease must try understanding that this disease is just like any other killer and should not be taken lightly. One must also understand it is unhealthy denying the truth of the matter. If you have a loved one with Alzheimer's, don't try convincing yourself it is just old age forgetfulness. Don't call them feeble and shrug it off. Take your loved one to a Neurologist and have the necessary tests done so you get a decent diagnosis. Denial of this disease will not help the person afflicted nor will it help you. What I am saying is shame or denial are not options with this disease.

Instead of looking at the disease as a societal stigma, look at it truthfully and treat it for what it is, a deterioration of brain cells caused either by a gene or the environment or both, but do not think of it as a shameful disease. It is just another disease like cancer and just as deadly except this disease has no cure.

It is also not a disease prevalent to old age; Alzheimer's can and will attack at any age, it just depends on conditions and whether your loved one has a predisposition to it.

Your first mistake will be underestimating the responsibilities associated with this disease. If you become the caregiver, your patient will cling to you as their total support. They will be so attached that even

three minutes out of their sight will create a panic situation on their behalf. Your patient might begin yelling, and quite loudly. When they see you, they will stop, and within minutes they will not remember the incident. If you ask them why they were yelling they might respond with something like, "I thought everyone was gone or dead. I thought I was all alone."

If you wait the few minutes after they quit yelling and ask that same question they will look at you with wonder; they will not remember the yelling part. This disease nearly eliminates the short-term memory right from the beginning of stage two. Actual memory loss begins in the early part of stage one but generally, the memory loss is insignificant and relatives tend to overlook it. A close relative might notice the subtle changes in their loved one but usually the changes are imperceptible. They might go unnoticed for two or more years.

Panic Attacks
Anxiety Attacks

You might also discover your patient's symptoms, when left alone, will cause a panic attack. There are a number of different manifestations of these attacks and they can be quite severe depending on your patient. The most common attack is increased heart rate, severe anxiety, sweating, intense fear, apprehension and a need to escape. I have even seen some patients vomit. You can almost always see the fear in their eyes.

If your patient begins yelling, that could be a type of panic attack manifested by fear. Your first experience with one might cause a panic attack in you. The patient will gasp for breath, shake all over and cry out as if in pain. You might think they are having a

heart attack but when you check their vital signs there will be nothing wrong. Blood pressure, pulse, and blood sugar levels will be normal. They might have a slightly elevated pulse but not always.

My mother-in-law scared the crap out of me on a number of occasions with her panic attacks. It was only after I began researching this disease that I discovered the cause of these attacks. As a caregiver, you must remember that fear is a terrible thing to live with and your Alzheimer's patient will live in nearly constant fear.

Once I discovered her anxiety caused these panic attacks I was able to cope with them and keep them at a minimum. Understanding what causes them helps.

I remember once I told mom we were planning a trip and later that day she began gasping for breath. I thought she was dying but as it turned out she was panicking. I think the idea of going on a trip upset her and I think she also thought she would be left behind. Either way, you will not be able to leave your patient for any more than two or three minutes at a time as they become frightened very easily and I suggest if you are planning any trips, you keep them to yourself. I found the best thing to do was simply put mom in the car and take off; I did not tell her we were going for a considerable distance. Since her memory was gone, she did not know how long we were in the car. When we returned from our trip, Florida to Niagara Falls, she had no memory of it.

It is important to note that there are drugs out there that will assist in the control of these attacks. Talk to your doctor about it; they can help.

Urgency to leave

Last night was interesting and quite heartbreaking at the same time. My mom suddenly decided it was time to go and she asked me when we were leaving. I replied. "There's no place to go, sweetheart. We are at home."

She got a quizzical look in her eyes and questioned. "We're home?"

I answered with a 'yes' and she quickly came back with. "Okay, then, let's go."

I again replied with, "We are home, mom. There is no place we can go. We have to stay here. We live here."

After she questioned our departure again, I tried a little more firmness but that did not work. My firmness created an atmosphere of argument and she became belligerent so I backed off and tried calming her.

Nothing seemed to work; I could see the anxiety building and I was quite helpless. After five years of dealing with this disease I still did not understand her suffering. I tried ignoring her and that only made matters worse. I decided the best approach was the quiet, calm, reserved mannerism. I would handle the incident with patience and love. We spent the next thirty minutes going over the same questions and answers until finally she began crying. I thought she was crying because I wouldn't get up out of the chair and leave but as it turned out she was crying because she suddenly realized she suffered from severe memory loss. She confessed she was scared and I said. "Here, take my hand. There is nothing to be frightened about. I am here."

"Then she replied. "I'm scared because I am afraid I will not remember anyone I love by morning."

I thought about her statement for a moment and then gave her the best answer I could. "By tomorrow you will be your old self and you will not remember this moment. Even if you forget all those who love you, they will still love you. I will still love you."

I thought my answer was sufficient and it did seem to calm her a little but what really worked was holding her and telling her we loved her.

After working with mom for the last five years I now understand that love does conquer all things. Our Alzheimer patients simply need love and reassurance that everything will be okay. I try to convince mom of that every day because telling her anything else only makes her sad and less communicative.

I discovered that stroking the side of her face soothes her and calms her. Also, holding her hand has a calming affect.

Fear of being alone

The fear of being alone is one of the symptoms of this disease and you will see it in your patient as the disease progresses. Even as I write this mom sits right next to me on the sofa and suffers from anxiety and panic attacks, all within the last ten minutes. She knows I am here but understands I am not giving her my undivided attention. Your patient will not allow you to ignore her or him. They will follow you from room to room and if you go outside they suffer severely. If you take them outside you will have to watch them every second.

We might not think of anxiety as a life threatening symptom but our patients' do and they will become fearful when they have an attack. The attacks

might begin in early stage two and will increase in severity as the disease develops. When I say this is a 24-hour a day job that is exactly what I mean. If you are not prepared to be supportive all day and all night you might have a panicked individual on your hands and sometimes those panic attacks are severe enough to cause your loved one to scream and yell as if they are dying.

Most of the anxiety our patients suffer is from being alone. I believe they get up at night because there is no one with them. One night I decided to stay in her room on a chair while she fell asleep and that worked out very well. The only problem with that is few of us are capable of sitting in a chair all night; we too must sleep. Last night I sat with her and held her hand until she went to sleep and that also worked out extremely well. I actually got two and half hours sleep.

It is impossible to be a great caregiver if you do not get enough sleep. If it is at all possible, I suggest you get someone to assist you at night; otherwise you will burn out and that means you are no good to yourself or your patient.

Sleepy all the time

You will also discover your patient will sleep a long time during the day—that is probably why they sometimes stay up all night. If you think you can keep them awake so they will sleep at night, well, all I can say is, 'good luck'. I have put a great deal of effort into keeping mom awake during the day so she will sleep better at night but to no avail. She falls asleep even while I am talking just to keep her awake. My wife says it is because I am boring, and tell the same stories over and over. Truthfully, your patient might sleep two or three hours in the daytime and maybe all night. On

the other hand, they might remain awake the entire day and do the same at night.

This disease is extremely unpredictable. Yet, all the symptoms you run into will be no different from other Alzheimer patients. The only difference from what I read and what I experience is the stage differences. I notice considerable overlapping of symptoms, but don't be fooled by un-matching symptoms; your patient will get worse and eventually they will not be able to continue.

Forgetting who you are

When your patient forgets who you are and begins screaming because he or she thinks you are a stranger or an intruder, this will be a challenging, chilling moment but you should not be alarmed at this symptom; Alzheimer patients forget everything as the disease progresses. If you are unable to handle the outburst then you might want to get assistance with your challenge. There are a number of facilities out there that will assist you in your care of your loved one. They do however, come with a large price tag. Some of those places charge as much as $50.00 an hour, just a little out of my price range.

Perhaps this will help. Nothing your Alzheimer patient thinks or does is permanent. The Alzheimer patient first suffers from loss of short-term memory that begins somewhere during second stage, possibility early third stage so, within minutes of conversations or incidences they will not remember them. Over time they lose their long-term memory and after that stage sets in, they will remember very little.

My mother-in-law just yesterday thought I was a stranger. She told my wife to get a hold of Ron and let him know what was going on. My wife, Darlene responded. "Ron is right here. He's holding your hand."

Mom looked at me and then turned back to Darlene and said. "Will you call him and tell him what is going on?"

Darlene replied. "Yes, I will call him."

Her answer satisfied mom and within a few seconds she turned to me and said. "You are so precious. I am glad you are here."

I asked her if she knew my name and she answered, "Your name is..." she hesitated and then went on, "Your name is Paul."

Paul was her brother's name. He died about ten years ago. I smiled and said. "We love you, mom."

There are two drugs that might help slow the process of dementia, Namenda and Aricept. These two drugs seem to be the ones that doctors recommend the most. I suggest you talk to your Neurologist about administering these drugs and I further suggest you do your own research on the side effects.

Namenda can and often does make the condition of Alzheimer's worse. If your patient is already very unsteady, Namenda might make him or her even more unsteady. You don't want your loved one falling and ending up in a hospital with broken bones so be very careful to watch for side effects.

I tried Namenda on mom and she stumbled and fell within a couple of hours after taking it. Not only did she fall, her memory seemed considerably worsened from the drug. Recently, I tried Aricept and that does seem to work a little better but even with Aricept I notice mom has some strange side effects. One of the side effects appears to be a more pronounced memory

loss and perhaps a little more agitated. It seemed when I had her on Aricept she became more argumentative. I did not want mom worsened by drugs so I discontinued the use of both Namenda and Aricept.

Mind you, none of these medicines have any long-term effect on this disease anyway so, if your patient has a negative reaction to any of them, I suggest you not use them. We have to remember that Alzheimer's has no cure and no real abatement so; any medicines available on the market today will not stop the disease. I personally do not like man-made medicines; they usually have serious side effects and sometimes those side effects can kill the patient.

Recently, my doctor prescribed a new medicine for me and I spent four days in the hospital with my blood pressure at 200/100. Medicines do not always help. I started taking a statin for my cholesterol and ended up lying on the floor unable to move.

Belligerence

Your patient may become belligerent and uncooperative.

You could find yourself in a position where your patient will remove all his or her clothes while in public. Not only is the situation embarrassing but also it may be construed as illegal. If your patient becomes belligerent at the same time, you might want to laugh at it rather than frustrate yourself with the details. You will probably find the situation difficult at best but not unmanageable.

While your patience is tested by the situation, it will behoove you to remain calm and try to keep your

patient dressed so as not to be completely embarrassed by the situation. However, if you find yourself in that predicament, good luck. I have been there a few times with mom and it is interestingly embarrassing, not to mention the stares you get from the watching public.

If a police officer should take note of your situation, it could be difficult explaining exactly what is going on. You might be able to explain that your patient suffers from Alzheimer's and maybe the officer will be satisfied with your explanation but it might not work for the curious bystanders. There are people who are unwilling to believe you have a patient with Alzheimer's and they will call the police with serious accusations. I have witnessed situations of this nature and found it curious that the caregiver had difficulty convincing the police he was only trying to get his patient's clothes back on. The witnesses said the caregiver was fighting with the patient and it appeared he was attempting an assault. Try not to get yourself into a situation of that nature. Accusations of this nature could be difficult to defend.

I suggest if your patient arrives at that stage of the disease you might consider professional help or possibly a care facility. The least you can do for your loved one is keep him or her safe in their surroundings. However, if you continue to take care of your patient on your own, you don't want to end up doing them a disservice. Just be sure you are not keeping them safe in your home environment for your own ego or your own peace of mind. Your peace of mind is not as important as your patient's well-being. Sometimes professional care is an important step in the right direction regardless of the costs.

I am not an advocate of nursing homes or assisted living facilities because I have this idea that I can do a better job of taking care of my mother-in-law

than anyone else on the planet. Naturally, that is my ego speaking. I am not a trained professional nor am I equipped with all the needed accessories required for an Alzheimer patient. It has taken me five years of study and working with this disease to actually get a feeling for how to handle it and I am still not a professional.

Sometimes it is prudent to ask for help and quite often that help is better equipped to handle your problem than you are. If you do not require any assistance then don't look for it. All I am suggesting is your patient might be difficult for you to handle and it is not shameful to ask for assistance.

Asking for help

If you have to leave your home for any length of time, it is better to get someone to come in and be a caregiver for a short period than take your patient out for long rides of long distant travel. Remember, it is not a bad thing to ask for help. Your Alzheimer patients may not do well with long periods in cars or planes; they become disoriented and confused. Sometimes that disorientation and confused state of mind can last for days. That is not a situation you want. Your patient is already disoriented and confused so it is not a good idea to make the condition worse.

I speak from experience. We took mom on a long vacation to Oregon and it was two or three weeks before she regained any semblance of orientation and I am not sure she has ever recovered.

When your patient begins showing a lack of cooperation or extreme disorientation, you might consider keeping them in a quiet atmosphere that is familiar to them rather than take them across the country. We knew her condition might worsen if we took the trip but her family wanted to see her.

However, if you constantly remove them from the home and take them places you will keep them in an agitated, confused state of mind and that is what they already suffer from, confusion and agitation.

Alzheimer patients do considerably better in familiar surroundings. Even if your patient does not recognize you, or the home they live in, it is still important for you as a caregiver to act normal and loving. They seem to respond to love much better than they do indifference or anger.

Loss of Communication Skills

You will notice, as I have, that your patient's vocabulary becomes limited to just a few words and that will begin in the middle of stage two. Alzheimer patients seem to lose their communication skills early. I don't know if the skills are lost because of something with the brain or if they just simply have no desire to communicate. Nearly every conversation you have with your patient will be one or two word answers on their part. They will offer limited responses that do not always make much sense. You might get a response like 'yes', when you ask a question. Yes might be the only word they know for a given day. I have heard mom say 'yes' to me for every question I had for an entire day and the next day she was giving me sentences. Sometimes the sentences are spastic unintelligible groups of words. Do not let that surprise you; Alzheimer patients do not always make sense with their responses.

I also discovered that mom will sit in a chair watching Television and think it is real. When I tell her it is just a fictitious story she will ask me if I know one of the actors. One day she asked me how many movies I

did with Humphrey Bogart. I did chuckle just a little about that one. I told her I was not an actor. After I told her I was not an actor she asked me if I knew Clint Eastwood. I said, "no, I do not know Clint. I wish I did but I don't"

She did not ask any questions about the subject any more that day but about four days later she went through it again and I had to tell her, 'no' all over again.

Chapter Three

Fear, Anxiety, Suspiciousness

Mom began showing signs of extreme fear and excessive anxiety in early stage three. Since there is no cure you can only reassure your loved one that he or she is loved and you are there for them. The symptoms do not last long but they are disturbing when they arrive.

Your doctor can and will prescribe some mild anxiety nighttime medicines that seem effective but I have to say these medicines do not always work; they help a little but not a lot.

I notice mom will sometimes remain in bed most of the night when I give her an anxiety pill, but they do not always keep her in bed. Last night she got up three times before midnight and at three AM: she piddled on the floor and then after I got that mopped up she decided it was time to get up for the day. There was no amount of talking or encouragement that changed her mind. In her mind it was time to get up and that is what she did. Naturally, I got up with her.

Some Alzheimer patients have tunnel vision, one-track minds, compulsive behavior that is impossible to deal with. You can't get mad at them and you can't control their behavior. All you can do is make them comfortable and hope they feel better. You will find as I stated, they suffer from short-term memory loss so their behavior will last a short period of time. In the mean time you must have patience and understanding.

You must also realize that while they suffer from short-term memory loss, they also suffer from complete, total memory loss as they go through the stages of this disease. You will see the deterioration as it progresses

and the loss of memory will continue until they can no longer function. They will even forget how to eat.

The other day I had to feed mom because she no longer understood the idea of a fork or a spoon. Recently, she did not recognize her coffee cup; she thought a book on the table was a cup. You should not let these moments surprise you. As the disease progresses and the memory of things slips away, all the things your patient used to do will disappear. You must prepare yourself for the inevitable. You must also understand that this disease will only get worse and if you are the caregiver, you must deal with it. There can be no place in your heart where you deny the inevitable. Don't try to fool yourself into believing they might get better; they will not.

Back when they thought this disease was the result of the patient being crazy or insane, they would lock them up and forget them, or beat them until they were bloody or dead. Knowing what I know now, I would love to go back in time and beat the hell out of their jailers. There is never an excuse for mistreating an Alzheimer's patient and there can be no excuse for cruelty to a mental patient. Anyone committing crimes of this nature should themselves be locked up.

Suspicious of You

Quite often your patient might become suspicious of you. This symptom can occur at any time and can occur sometimes more than once during a day or night. They simply do not recognize you and that scares them. You must remember that this disease is a disease of the brain and as the brain deteriorates the patient's memory loss becomes greater. It is heartbreaking but a natural course of the disease. They will eventually forget everything as time passes and the

final stage of the disease is not one I want to watch and neither do you. However, the moments where they forget who you are might only last for a few minutes and then everything will be fine again until the next episode.

Mom no longer recognizes my name but she still recognizes me. If I ask her who I am she will not remember and she cannot respond to the question. In fact, she rarely ever responds to a question. If I ask her who she is, she will sometimes respond with her name. She no longer remembers her marriage of fifty plus years and she has difficulty remembering her children.

She still remembers one of her brothers, the one who took care of her when she suffered from Encephalitis. Encephalitis is a disease she had prior to her teen years. Encephalitis is often called, 'Brain Fever' because of the excessive body temperature suffered by the victim. 'Brain Fever' comes from the sting of a mosquito carrying the disease.

Mom's Neurologist believes her Alzheimer's started earlier in her life because of that problem when she was a little girl. She told me she was in a hospital for over a year from the Encephalitis. I am willing to believe her Neurologist in this matter.

Now, even her childhood is a vague memory and while she still remembers having a disease, she no longer remembers exactly what it was. If I remind her she will respond with a, "Oh, yes", but I doubt she remembers. I think she is responding to a question with an affirmative answer because I expect an answer.

The final stages of this disease, where your patient becomes more reliant for his or her daily needs, presents difficult times. They become less responsive to stimulus and less cognitive of their surroundings. When that time comes it might behoove you and even me to consider assisted living arrangements or perhaps a

Hospice. Either way, our loved ones with Alzheimer's will be cared for and we all want the best for our patients.

I am sure when mom gets to the point where she can no longer get out of bed, I will have to put her in the care of professionals. I can honestly say I am not looking forward to that time so I will probably place her in the care of professionals before we get to that point.

Loss of Motor Skills

Mom suffers from severe loss of motor skills, loss of balance and an inability to support herself without assistance. Sometimes she can't walk and if there is any distance to the walk we put her in a wheel chair.

Alzheimer patients become short of breath in late stage three, early stage four and they generally do not get better once these symptoms show themselves. However, I have seen mom show signs of improvement for short periods and sometimes she walks quite well. Not every patient follows the rules of the disease exactly the same.

Another noticeable symptom that I see manifesting its ugly head is constant shaking. Mom now shakes while sitting, walking, or just standing in one spot. The shaking is uncontrollable. Then again, the shaking seems to come and go without any regularity. Naturally, the shaking is a sign of the nervous system breaking down. She has had this symptom for the last two months but today she shows no signs of shaking. In fact, she seems quite normal. The only problem I see is, when I ask her to tell me her name she has no response.

I remember how vigorous she was just a few years ago and now watching her is very difficult. She used to help her husband chop down the trees around

our property. I watched her move logs and dig holes—she was tough.

Even though there are times when mom appears a little better, the symptoms still get worse and more frequent. No matter how she appears in her environment, she still has to be helped around the house, in and out of cars and up and down curbs. She has considerable difficulty standing up from a chair. I also notice she has completely lost her depth perception at night. When she walks at night she feels her way along and shows considerable anxiety about her footing. If the color of the walkway changes, she will stop and refuse to move for fear of falling. I have tried to get her to take a step but she refuses; the ground changes color and in her mind it looks like a giant drop-off.

One thing you will find with your patient or other patients is they hate to be in one place for any length of time. You might put your patient in a chair, turn your back and within two minutes he or she will be up and out of sight. If you leave your doors open, I suggest you close them; Alzheimer patients have been known to walk right out of the house and not be found for hours, even days, sometimes not found alive. Our patients have no understanding of the world or how big it is outside.

There is also the compulsion to sleep, not just during the day but sometimes your patient will sleep well past 9:00 AM. I have on a number of occasions awakened mom just so she will not sleep the entire day. I doubt it would hurt her to sleep all day but then she would definitely be up all night.

Compulsive Behavior

If you watch your patient for different behavior patterns you will discover that he or she will do things over and over, like button a blouse or a sweater. Most of the time mom has no ability to button her blouses; she will unbutton them but will not be able to button them back up. I watch her undo the buttons on her blouse ten or twenty times while sitting in a chair and most of those times she will be unable to correctly place the buttons back into their respective holes. I will do it for her because she gets agitated if the task becomes impossible. I do not like her in an agitated state of mind so I take the time to show her how to re-button her blouse.

On a couple of occasions I put a pull over blouse on her but that tended to cause more frustration. I imagine because the pullover blouse has no buttons she did not understand it. I think in her mind all blouses had to have buttons. I discovered the cure for that was to put a blouse with buttons over the pullover blouse and then let her fiddle with the buttons. As long as she does not become frustrated I leave her alone.

The other day I watched her try to tie the tails of her robe together like the girls in school used to do with the tails of their blouses; they would tie them together around their midriffs. I watched as mom attempted to tie the ends of a thick robe together. I tried explaining to her that it couldn't be done but she refused to listen and finally accomplished the tie. Not only did she get the tie completed, she double tied the ends. She is very persistent when she wishes to accomplish something. I think telling our patients they cannot do something is an exercise in futility on our part. Alzheimer patients do what they want to do for any given moment.

Compulsive behavior is just another symptom that you most likely will experience. It will do you no good to make any attempt to stop whatever behavior your patient decides needs accomplishing. When they begin doing something, they will not hear anything you say and even if they do hear you, they will not respond. Mom will say, "Yes" to me as if she understands but will continue right on with the chosen behavior for that moment. The only thing you can do is let your patient continue as long as their behavior is not injurious to themselves or others. You will notice when they respond to your voice with a yes, they actually do not understand your question or statement.

Every so often she will forget who I am and that can become a difficult time for both her and me, not because I am frustrated but because she becomes frustrated trying to get me out of her face. She doesn't know who I am and as far as she's concerned, I am an intruder. She will try hitting or struggle with me while I am attempting to help her. She simply does not understand the reason for me being there and like most Alzheimer patients, she can and will put up a fight. I find the best thing to do in the moment, if she is not in danger, is just let her be. Ten minutes later she will be okay.

Cold All the Time

I know our elderly have lost much of their subcutaneous layer of fat called the hypodermis and that contributes to the condition of being cold all the time, but your Alzheimer patient might be suffering from brain damage in that area that controls body temperature and in mom's case she is freezing cold all the time. Her metabolism is changing every day and lately she complains she is cold even at 80 degrees. I

can pile the clothes on her and she will still sit in a chair and shiver. I imagine what happens is the brain cells running the internal thermostat are deteriorating so certain controls are shutting down causing the body to no longer respond to external heating stimulus. For you as the caregiver, this will mean your patient might require a sweater or a coat for five minutes and then tell you he or she is hot and the sweater or coat will be removed. Ten minutes later you might be replacing it. There is no determining what the internal thermostat will tell your patient at any given moment.

Look out for Poop

I would use a more sophisticated word but I have to apologize for my bluntness. When you get out of bed in the morning and you find feces smeared all over your patient's bedroom, on the walls, saturated all over the floor completely imbedded into the carpet, then you have to be aware of the Poop. By the way, if you have a very light colored carpet in your patient's room, you might want to cover it with some protective cloth like a painter's cloth.

If it wasn't such a tragedy, I think a good chuckle would be in order but in our case, I can only feel the pain of my mother-in-law when she knows how much control she has lost of her own body. Usually, after those times when she has no control over her bowel movements, she will cry for a time. I try to comfort her and that does seem to work. We, as caregivers can be thankful for their memory loss because within an hour most patients will forget those times of distress.

Alzheimer patients have no idea what they are doing most of the time when they arrive near the end of stage two and definitely no cognitive powers in stages

beyond three. They can and will do just about anything a child will do and they seem to be better at it.

As the brain deteriorates, it appears from my observations, that our patients revert back to some age around two or there. They actually do not know what they are doing and they might say or do anything on the spur of the moment. You might find your patient naked in front of your house or when company comes they might just take off their clothes. If your visitors are open minded it might not be embarrassing but I find it a little discomforting when mom decides it is too hot in the house. Normally, she thinks it is cold even at 80 degrees or higher but if she suddenly decides it is hot she will begin removing her clothes and it will not matter who happens to be visiting at the time.

Mom has difficulty at night finding a bathroom and I discovered sometime ago, you never close the door and turn off all the lights. The caregiver creates disasters if the caregiver does not understand this disease. If you turn off all the lights in your patient's bedroom and close the doors you might find a very distasteful prize around the room in the morning. Your patient must have the freedom to walk around a little; else confining them to a small room could be disastrous. I know in those homes where they care for Alzheimer patients they have to keep them in their rooms at night but in your own home it might be best to let them wander just a little. I discovered keeping mom confined is not a good thing when it comes to her moods.

I would also suggest if your patient shows any predisposition toward allergenic reactions to certain foods like ice cream, you might refrain from feeding that substance to him or her. Mom is somewhat allergic to ice cream and she craves it all the time, as do many Alzheimer patients. Every time I relent and let her eat it, I have a disaster in the morning. Let me remind you,

her room is carpeted. If you value your carpets or any belongings that might be in your patient's room you might want to consider the consequences of diarrhea.

I suggest you watch your patient and make some attempt at controlling his or her diet and keep some Imodium on hand just in case of emergencies. I don't know why but Alzheimer patients seem to have frequent diarrhea. Believe me when I tell you antidiarrheal medicines actually do work.

Early Stage Alzheimer Patients

Early stages of Alzheimer's can be diagnosed in some, but not every individual with these symptoms of forgetfulness can be diagnosed as having Alzheimer's and quite often a person suffering from severe dementia is not an Alzheimer's patient at all. In my mother-in-law's case we took her to a Neurologist and after a brain scan he told us she suffered from White matter deterioration. Most Alzheimer's patients suffer from gray matter deterioration so his diagnosis excluded the word, 'Alzheimer's' from his list.

I believe his diagnosis excluded naming her condition with an exclusive disease was because she had no gray matter deterioration and declaring an individual has Alzheimer's is the same as giving them a death sentence. Therefore, he elected to say she suffered from moderate to severe Dementia. It is an excellent escape word covering all bases. You might notice doctors do not like diagnosing your loved one with Alzheimer's.

Usually, Friends, family or co-workers begin noticing a close relative displaying difficulties such as forgetfulness or behavioral changes. Quite often a detailed medical interview will disclose problems with memory or concentration. If you take your loved one to his or her regular doctor the doctor can perform some

simple tests and make recommendations conducive to his or her condition.

When questioned, mom had considerable difficulty remembering things that happened just a day prior. On different occasions she would ask me who I was and I would go through a long explanation as to what my role was regarding her. I would tell her I was her caregiver, the individual who took care of her. Her memory was bad enough that she could not remember how she came to live in my home. I would take the time to explain to her how her daughter and I brought her to our home after her husband died. It seemed my explanations always satisfied her questions but only for a short period of time.

There are times when mom will ask the same question over and over as many as twenty or thirty times within ten seconds of each other. I discovered the best way to handle the questions was to answer them completely each time she asked. It does no good to say things like, "I just told you the answer to that question ten seconds ago…" If you become snippy with the patient, your patient might feel as if you are mad at them and then they will respond with depression or anger and even fear. It is better to continue answering their questions no matter how many times they ask and always do it in a kind manner. Yes, it takes considerable patience and yes, you must always be gentle, quiet and compassionate.

You might find your patient wandering around at night and it is possible they might tell you it is time to get out of here or it is time to go. They might tell you that someone is coming and "…we must run away…" If you ask them who is coming they will not give you a reasonable answer. I tell mom, when she has those types of dreams that I am here to protect the family and no one can hurt anyone as long as I am here. That

usually settles her down and I can almost always get her back to bed. Quite often when I get her back to bed she remains there for a couple of minutes and then she is back up wandering around. I have a medicine that her doctor prescribed that seems to work quite well. It calms her fears and helps her sleep but even the medicine does not always work.

I also discovered it is a good idea to close and lock all the doors in the house at night except her bedroom door and the bathroom doors. If you do not close all the doors in the house your patient might mistake a room like your pantry for a bathroom; you might have a surprise waiting for you in the morning.

If your patient does not wear protective panties or shorts, that surprise will go all through the house. If you have carpeted rooms, you may want to consider some carpet protectors or perhaps a product you can put on your patient for protecting your home from his or hers incontinence. Our floors are tile and easy to clean but it still takes considerable time to clean all the rooms mom visits during the night. Those of you with carpet will have your work cut out for you if you do not take precautions for protection.

I also find it interesting that we have four bathrooms in our home and mom usually does not find even one of them.

I received one of those surprises this morning at 6:00AM. It took me until 11:05AM before I finished with her shower, carpet cleaning and bed clothes. Yes, we did purchase a carpet-cleaning machine with the idea in mind that mom has a considerable number of accidents.

I suggest you get yourself a carpet cleaner a little better than the rental type. The rental ones do not get your carpet as clean as those with built in heaters. Hot water coming from the carpet cleaner seems to work a

little better than cold. I also discovered some of those liquids that you buy from the potpourri section at Wal-Mart help cover any odors that might linger. Another product I put in the water is a very small amount of bleach for sterilization purposes. If you do put bleach in your cleaner, you want to be sure it is a small amount and don't blame me if it ruins your carpet. Carpets do not generally care much for bleach. So be very careful with those types of products.

Music Always Helps

Music or just their favorite radio station seems to be a soothing stimulus. Alzheimer patients, while not remembering things still remember beautiful music.

Mom loves classical music and as a pianist I can play a number of classical pieces, so I will play while she sits in a chair and listens. Now, this does not always work; there are times when she complains about the stereo or the piano but for the most part she will quietly listen to music.

I am convinced mom no longer understands exactly what comes from the TV. She sits and watches but the other day while watching a Sit-Com she became scared and anxious. I asked what was wrong and she said, "That thing scares me."

"I inquired, "The TV?"

She replied. "Yes."

I immediately grabbed the remote and turned it off. I decided it is best not to react with emotion to her outbursts. Reacting to her outbursts with any excitement or show of emotion causes the incident to worsen.

Alzheimer patients understand your emotions and they will react to them sometimes with violence or extreme fear. Your best bet is to act perfectly calm and

in complete control. That usually settles them down. Arguing with them only accelerates the anxiety and makes the incidence worse. Mom can and will become argumentative if I or anyone else tries to change her mind about something. Once in the doctor's office she let out an outburst of flowery words. The doctor looked at her and said, "My, my. Aren't we feeling cheery today?"

Mom replied with "I don't give a Damn!"

I immediately thought of Walter the puppet.

Mom's demeanor changes from moment to moment and if she decides on something like removing her clothes, well, all I can say is, 'She has interesting moments".

You will find these same symptoms in your patient and if you take them with a grain of salt, you will handle those situations without too much difficulty.

One more fascinating thing I discovered about our patients is this; if they do something wrong you might find your patient will blame you for the wrongdoing. They might mischievously make a mess and then claim it was someone else who did it.

Chapter Four

Handling Your Alzheimer's Patient

If you are currently a caregiver for an individual with Alzheimer's you might wonder about the disease the same as I wonder. If you have been a caretaker for a period of time, you certainly understand the frustrations that go along with the disease, not just to you but to the patient as well. This disease is quite demanding of the caregiver's time and demanding to the patient who knows and understands they are losing their mind or as I tell mom; "You are not losing your mind; you are losing your memory".

I can only imagine what goes through their minds as they see their world slip away. That is why we caregivers must be full of compassion. We are their only support. When you feel like you want to explode you must still handle any and all situations with a calm deliberate attitude. Your patient needs your love and your understanding not your outbursts of emotion. Even when they do not know who you are, you must still give them your love and your support. I find caressing mom's cheek with the back of my hand has a very soothing effect on her and whenever she gets anxious or scared I use that technique.

My mother-in-law's name is Betty and I call her 'Mom'. She goes through some very difficult nights, some are quite difficult for me and heartbreaking at the same time but we get through them. I find every day a little different and a little more challenging.

The first time I met Betty was thirty years ago in 1982. Before I married her daughter, Darlene. Darlene

wanted me to meet her parents before we married and that is always a good idea. Most of us understand that meeting parents for the first time can go just about any direction. Because I am 17 years older than Darlene, Betty was quite suspicious of my intentions. Since I am a perceptive sort of fellow I could tell after a few minutes she was not too fond of me. I found a moment when I could talk to her alone and took her aside and quietly said. "I will never hurt your daughter and I will never leave her if we marry."

My statement immediately eased the tension but she was still suspicious. Over the years she relaxed quite a bit toward me and after ten years or so, she actually began to tolerate me. Mind you, I did not say she liked me but she did tolerate me.

I think mom began loosening up after my father-in-law retired and bought a travel trailer. They set out on an exploratory journey that took them around the country including Canada and Alaska. After they traveled around for a few months they finally settled their little RV on our property in Live Oak, Florida. I hooked up a sewer system and they lived there on our property for several years.

During their stay, I went through bypass surgery and I actually think mom worried about my recovery. However, much to everyone's chagrin, I did recover sufficiently and life continued on as if nothing ever happened, well, I fake it well.

My wife wanted to finish her bachelor's degree in accounting so we sold our Live Oak home and moved to Jacksonville, Florida where she attended UNF. Meanwhile mom and dad moved back to Bend Oregon where they settled down in a small apartment.

In January 2007, dad died and the family decided mom should come live with my wife and me in Jacksonville. Mom also agreed to the arrangement. She liked it in

Bend and she enjoyed living with her son, David, but she also wanted to get away from some old memories.

I had to go to Bend and get her car because she could no longer drive. Darlene and I decided we needed a car so I flew back to Bend, Oregon and got the car. Driving it back to Jacksonville gave mom a chance to visit and see if she really wanted to live with us so she rode along with me. During that rip we got to know each other and I think she actually began liking me.

It was during that drive across the country that I first noticed she had some minor difficulties with her cognition. At one point during the journey, I handed her a map and put my finger on the spot where we were and asked her to tell me the distance to the next exit. She had no idea what my question entailed and she could not give me a reasonable answer. She studied the map for a few moments and then replied. "I can't tell from this thing where we are."

I thought about her answer for a moment and then replied. "I'll stop up here at the next rest area and we'll figure it out there."

I did not think too much about the incident but I remembered how she related her Alaska trip with her husband, my father-in-law and she specifically told me she was the navigator on that trip. Obviously, her map reading skills deteriorated considerably over those few years. At that time I made no connection relating her inability to read a map with that of Alzheimer's. I remember a number of individuals in the military who could not read a map even after a map reading class. Reading or recognizing map related positions while driving is not that easy anyway so I didn't really give it much thought.

I shrugged off the incident and gave it no more consideration because she acted and seemed perfectly normal. I did not consider map reading an important

part of functionality. It was two years later when the map reading incident came back to the forefront when I discovered she could not remember what cities she lived in. She would ask me if she still worked and she had difficulty remembering some of the places she lived. I finally required of her doctor about her condition and he recommended a Neurologist. The Neurologist told me she suffered from moderate dementia.

Her moderate dementia appeared to be just that, moderate dementia. He did note a deterioration of the white matter in her brain. Now we are finding out that new investigations into white brain matter suggest that Alzheimer's might actually begin in the white matter instead of the gray matter. There are a few studies being conducted as a result of these findings.

Many doctors and researchers suggest that mom's inability to read that map was stage one of Alzheimer's; it's a stage of the disease that shows few and often times no symptoms, and for the purpose of this writing, I will also conclude that incident and a few others that I noticed as the beginnings of this disease.

It is important to note that even her Neurologist three years later did not brand her as an Alzheimer's patient; he called her condition 'Mild Dementia'. I actually got the impression he was surprised to find no apparent deterioration of her gray matter showed up in her brain scan. It is possible that he had heard nothing about the research being done on the White Matter as a possible link to Alzheimer's. Even doctors do not always keep up with research.

I also did not give much consideration to Alzheimer's when the Neurologist used the word 'Dementia' but later I discovered the severity of her dementia went considerably deeper than just a mild loss of memory; mom suffered from something much worse.

I spent considerable time around patients in nursing homes and homes for the elderly when I played the piano publicly and I never came across any patient with mom's level of memory loss. Yet, according to my studies, Alzheimer's was identified as an individual disease about 100 years ago. Individuals suffering from the disease, before its identification, received labels such as, 'crazy', 'stupid', 'demented', 'insane', 'possessed' and other derogatory handles, none of which identified the disease properly. We now know these people are not crazy or possessed but suffer from an abnormal gene that plays havoc with their memory.

This is not a disease of shame; it is a disease that attacks brain cells just like cancer attacks the cells of your body. A person suffering from Alzheimer's should not be shunned or laughed at, but rather, they should be loved and cared for. This is not a disease we run from but a disease we work with in order to make our patient comfortable.

When I take mom out in public, I am not ashamed of her condition; I simply tell the curious she suffers from Alzheimer's. I have not found one person yet who backed of or ran away in fear. Alzheimer's is just another disease and should be treated as such.

Visible Alzheimer's

Mom moved in with my wife and me in September of 2007, seven months after her husband, my father-in-law, died. At the time, she was 73 years old. It was a year and a half later when the doctor told me she suffered from 'Mild Dementia'. By the time she reached 76, she was in stage two of Alzheimer's and her memory loss was considerable.

There was a time during mom's third year with us where her symptoms worsened. We were at the

kitchen table discussing lunch when she suddenly questioned. "Are the police looking for you?"

The question surprised me because it came right out of the midst of a conversation about lunch. I replied, "No, the police are not looking for me. Why are you asking me a question like that?"

"Because you brought me here, I thought everyone would be worried. Someone must have called the police by now."

I realized her mind had slipped just a little and replied. "Mom, you're seventy six years old, not thirteen or fourteen. The police are not looking for you nor are they looking for me."

"Then who are you?" she questioned.

"I'm Ron, your son-in-law. You live here with me and your daughter."

She sat there for a few moments and then answered. "So, I live here. How did I get here?"

I spent the next hour explaining how she came to live with us and explained her age and her past. Just for that moment she forgot everything about her past and reverted back to her childhood. At that particular moment, she was only twelve or thirteen.

I never experienced a situation of that nature before and mom never showed any signs of mental deterioration of that magnitude. I thought she suffered from a mild form of Dementia.

After that I went to the Internet and began reading up on dementia. My reading took me to the symptoms of Alzheimer's and its stages. That's when I realized mom didn't just suffer from some sort of mild dementia; she had Alzheimer's.

Alzheimer's is not just some ordinary disease one gets as they age; Alzheimer's is a cruel, debilitating, catastrophic calamity for the patient and the family. When I discussed mom's dementia with her doctor, he

did confirm that she might be suffering from the disease but I could tell he was unwilling to put a label on her condition other than Dementia. Actually, he did not confirm she suffered from Alzheimer's it until I pointed it out and even then he did not actually say she had the disease.

Can it be cured?

No! We have no cure for the disease at this time. There are a number of research programs currently looking at the disease but they have not found a cure.

I have my own beliefs about the disease, where it comes from and why some people get it while others do not but then all our diseases appear to be selective when they attack.

As I said in my opening statement, I believe many of the diseases we experience today are man made or enhanced by our environment from our food preservatives or possibly Fluorides or gene defects but none of those individuals doing research has come up with a solution and they are quick to deny it as a man-made disease. No one in the food industry or in the government will admit that certain chemicals or food preservatives could be and probably are detrimental to our health. Not one person in government will ever say anything bad about fluorides, yet fluorides are considerably more dangerous than any Florida sun. The Food and Drug Association is just now requiring toothpaste with fluoride to carry a danger label. That should tell parents something. Just one drop of fluoride can kill and fluoride poisoning is deadly enough to almost always be fatal. The truth about fluoride can be found on the Internet. I suggest you not believe everything you read about this chemical but at least

prepare yourself for some understanding of what we put up with everyday in our food supply and other chemicals shoved down our throats.

Medicines?

There are a few medicines out there that doctors prescribe but I have tried them on mom and as I mentioned earlier, Namenda makes her worse. The following are the current medicines and if you have an Alzheimer's patient you might want to ask your doctor about them. I discovered that while they show promise and have medicinal value they could make your patient dizzy and prone to falling, so be careful when using them. Drugs that make a condition worse tend to scare the crap out of me. I have talked to other people who are caregivers and they say the drugs work very well. I am slightly more skeptical than most. Personally, I am not a person who cares that much for drugs especially when they appear to make a condition worse. For your information, the following are the drugs currently in use for Alzheimer patients.

1: Acetylcholinesterase inhibitors---ARICEPT: (donepezil HCl), approved to treat all stages of Alzheimer's disease. This particular drug I administered to mom and frankly, I believe it made her condition worse. I noticed her level of discomfort increased and her cognitive reasoning appeared better but her mood swings changed and she became irritated quicker. Perhaps all that was just my imagination but I took her off the medicine because I noticed those subtle changes.

2: EXELON: (rivastigmine tartrate), approved to treat mild to moderate Alzheimer's disease. I have not tried this one.

3: EXELON PATCH: (rivastigmine transdermal system), approved to treat mild to moderate Alzheimer's disease. Haven't tried this one either.

4: RAZADYNE: (galantamine HBr), approved to treat mild to moderate Alzheimer's disease. Have not tried this one.

5: NAMENDA: is currently the only drug of its type approved to treat moderate to severe Alzheimer's disease. This particular drug is the one that actually appeared to make mom's condition much worse. Shortly after she took the drug she fell down and I noticed her cognition deteriorated rapidly.

Some Symptoms You Might Notice

As you might suspect, although first stage symptoms are not usually noticeable, a good observer will see changes in their loved one suffering from this dreaded disease. You might think the changes are just old age forgetfulness but if you are up on the subject you will recognize the disease.

Your patient may forget how to count backwards or he or she might have difficulty with simple math problems. Inability to solve simple problems is among the first signs of the disease. Loss of short-term memory is an early stage sign of this disease. Your patient might suddenly forget how to operate a microwave and then suddenly figure it out. You might not even notice the symptom. Another symptom not so noticeable is your patient's loss of balance.

Many Alzheimer patients do not show this symptom in the first two stages but sometimes a loss of balance will begin in stage one. When a person reaches age thirty, most begin losing their balance when they close their eyes, especially if they attempt standing on

one foot. Your Alzheimer patient will begin losing their balance even with their eyes open and if you watch your loved one closely, you might see this symptom as early as stage one, they might be in that stage before they reach age 70. I have met individuals with Alzheimer's as young as fifty.

Most patients try to hide their symptoms because of embarrassment or fear. When our near relatives or our loved ones begin showing signs of their old age, they fear we might put them in nursing homes or worse so they pretend there is nothing wrong.

Patients in the early stages of the disease might forget how to wash dishes or dress themselves. They will begin to fail at simple tasks. Their uncertainty about their balance might make them prone to falling. My mother-in-law weighs over 150 lbs. and being 75 years old myself I find it quite difficult getting her back on her feet after she takes a tumble. Naturally, you don't want anyone falling even at a young age but us older individuals tend to break more easily than the young ones; our bones are not as strong as our younger generation counterparts so we might break from our fragility.

Your patient will show signs of difficulty with time concepts. They will not understand complex directions, especially if you give your patient more than one direction at a time. They will have difficulty with spatial concepts. Your patient will show signs of disinterest in conversation; they will become more reclusive. They will begin displaying mood swings that can be difficult for the caregiver to understand. They may have difficulty remembering their bedroom or the bathroom. They will probably forget family members in the early stages but those symptoms come and go with your patient's level of exhaustion. That is, if you tire your patient with too much activity, they will most

likely suffer severe memory loss for a day or two. Vacations have debilitating consequences with this disease.

Chapter Five

Noticeable Stages of Alzheimer's

Stage One

My private, non-professional research into this disease shows there are six stages of deterioration. Some doctors and hospitals show seven stages while others show only three. In the seven-stage model, the first stage has no noticeable symptoms. However, the six stage and models showing only three stages show stage one with symptoms. Therefore I will use the seven-stage model for this book because after taking care of mom for nearly six years I have watched her progression with this disease and I think the seven-stage model more clearly shows how the symptoms develop. So, when you look up the disease you will see all the different models and if you are like me, you will choose the seven-stage model to study. That model will help you with your understanding of this disease.

Some people show signs of dementia even in their forties. I believe I began showing signs of dementia in my late sixties. Now I am near 76 and will be 76 before I finish this book. My memory is not so good. I do not show signs of Alzheimer's but old age dementia can be quite frustrating. However, do not confuse ole age dementia with Alzheimer's; they are completely disassociated diseases showing similar symptoms.

Alzheimer's Stage One

The patient begins showing actual signs of memory loss or sudden changes in personality characteristics. Some of these changes are noticeable but the layperson may not associate them with senility or dementia, especially Alzheimer's. Often times these changes are mistaken for just plain old forgetfulness. My own mother showed signs of dementia as early as her thirtieth birthday. We called her forgetful but never thought of her as having a condition. Yet, as I think back on my mother's condition, I realize she had severe dementia. She died at an early age so she never had to go through any conditions of complete memory loss. With your own patient or relative in mind, you might notice a mild decline in their cognitive powers and sometimes in older women there will be an increased interest in sex. Since most women in their seventies have gone through menopause, individuals associated with the patient might be surprised at the sudden interest in sex, but most elderly women do not broadcast their renewed discovery of sex; they keep the symptoms to themselves.

I would think a woman in her seventies finding themselves suddenly interested in sex would find the condition embarrassing. That might explain why they seldom mention these newly found sex drives.

I discovered that few doctors associate renewed sex drives in elderly women as having anything to do with Alzheimer's or even dementia. However, they do appear to be associated with something happening to the brain that affects the hormone balance in the patient. I found when I mentioned mom's newly found interest in sex; her doctor immediately gave

consideration to Tertiary syphilis. Her doctor ordered blood tests for discovery of that disease but did not find anything supportive of her conclusions.

When her doctor ruled out anything to do with Syphilis she appeared to have no idea why mom had a new found interest in men. Had she done a brain scan at that time, she might have discovered considerable white matter deterioration, which could have led to a diagnosis. Consequently, her not doing a brain scan at that time left mom's Alzheimer's a question of simple dementia for more than two years.

I do not find it unusual that doctors look for causes other than dementia for increased sex drives in older women because doctors are cause oriented. Many doctors, while understanding that dementia or Alzheimer's are real diseases do not look at those diseases for symptomatic causes. They like to find real solutions while not understanding that Alzheimer's is a real solution that can and often does produce symptoms masking other diseases.

Chapter Six
Stage Two
When Symptoms become noticeable

In the beginning of stage two of Alzheimer's, patients find counting backwards by seven quite difficult. Mom found it difficult to count backwards by any number and simple math problems were beyond her. The problems with her symptoms were they could be related to normal aging, which meant a diagnosis of Alzheimer's was not on the top of the list.

None of the doctors we visited wanted to say she had Alzheimer's so we had no diagnosis for the beginnings of stage two for nearly a year and as I pointed out previously, doctors don't like those labels. I would imagine they do not like labeling individuals with the disease because of the stigma associated with it. Some people still believe that Alzheimer patients are crazy or possessed.

I think we are safe in ruling out the supernatural nonsense, the crazy theory and other theories that have no basis in fact. Alzheimer's is a real disease and it is possible to do certain tests on an individual and discover any predisposition for the disease. It does run in families and it is a gene that carries the disease and while it cannot be cured it can be discovered.

As with other Alzheimer patients, mom knew she suffered from minor memory loss. There were familiar words she could no longer remember. Incidentally, I have the same problem. Mom would also forget the location of things like her clothes or the closet they hung in. Sometimes she could not find her bedroom. On

several occasions she asked where she could find the bathroom. All of these symptoms were signs of forgetfulness but not necessarily signs of Alzheimer's. In addition, when mom forgot the location of her bedroom she would enter our bedroom and actually try to get in our bed. Either my wife or I would have to get up and take her to her own bed. In the morning she would have no memory of the incident.

Common stage two difficulties include:

Patient develops problems coming up with the correct word

Mom developed difficulties remembering what word she should use for a given moment. Quite often she would not remember a person's name, a person she knew for many years. I also noticed during the second stage of the disease that while mom was fantastic at answering Jeopardy questions, her ability to do so diminished rapidly. At the beginning of her second stage development she could no longer answer Jeopardy questions. She still watches the program but now she says nothing in response to the answers.

Mom also has trouble remembering names when introduced to new people. When introduced to a person mom would not remember that person ten minutes later. She would even ask them who they were almost immediately after being introduced. I also noticed that she would fake her understanding of situations by carefully choosing her words so as to give the impression she was perfectly normal. This attempt on her part to appear normal is a symptom of the disease.

Unsuspecting individuals would think her perfectly normal on first meeting. However, Alzheimer patients give themselves away by over reacting to situations. They tend to be a bit more (huggy) and a little more friendly than a normal individual. Mom would literally hug a perfect stranger and talk to the Wal-Mart greeter for two or three minutes. She would say things like, "you are doing a wonderful job…" or "I am so glad to see you again…" These catch phrases pop out of her mouth as if they are normal responses to a given situation, but as the caregiver, I can tell mom is simply reliving moments where individuals from her past said the same words to her and now she repeats them.

I also noticed that mom lost her ability to write letters. She had a longtime friend that worked with her at K-Mart and they communicated for many years after mom retired. Sometime early in stage two of her disease she quit writing to her friend. Later I wrote letters for her but she eventually forgot her friend's name and their association.

Alzheimer patients have noticeably greater difficulty performing tasks in social or work settings. They can forget material they read within minutes of reading it and they find it difficult relating to fellow employees. They might actually forget a long-time co-worker. This goes along with all the other symptoms of forgetfulness. Alzheimer's patients generally do not remember anything short-term.

I have talked to mom on several occasions about her short-term memory being gone and she accepts the disability but she also questions me about being embarrassed for her. I always assure her that nothing she could do would embarrass me. You might also notice that your patient might forget how to read or show signs of reading very slowly and stammering through even small words.

Losing or Misplacing Valuable Objects

This, I found is also a common problem with Alzheimer patients. Mom lost credit cards, ID cards and other important documents. Once she lost her identification and her Medicare cards. It took over three months to replace them. Actually, I think she threw them away because she thought she no longer needed them. When your patient is in stage two you must be aware of his or her lack of understanding the value of identification. You may have to take complete charge of your loved ones life. I suggest you remove from your patient's possession all their personal information along with all their credit cards.

It is suggested you give your patient an identification bracelet in the event they wander off. Mom has wandered away from me on three or four occasions but that was when she could still answer her phone. She no longer remembers what a phone is and when her phone rings; she has no clue about answering it. She will hand it to me because it is too complicated for her. As a result of her inability to comprehend the phone as a mechanism I removed it from her possession. This does place an extra burden on me because now I dare not let her out of my sight.

Alzheimer patients, when they wander off have no idea where they are going or why they are leaving. I suspect they are looking for something but since we do not know their age at any given moment, we have no idea where their mind takes them. When I say I do not know her age at any given moment, I mean she sometimes thinks she is a little girl again and lives

within that dream for as much as twenty or thirty minutes.

I asked her once where she thought she was going and she replied, "I have to get home."

I found her answer interesting but since she lived with me, I thought she might have reverted back to some earlier age, like thirteen or so and realized she had to get home before her father came home from work. I only say that because she told me that once in a conversation. She said, "Well, I have to get home before dad gets there."

Increased difficulties planning or organizing.

Alzheimer patients are incapable of planning a day. They lose their organizational skills almost within the first year of their infirmity. In the last year mom has gotten out of bed somewhere around midnight, dressed herself completely, picked up her purse and announced she was going to work. She has done that over one hundred times in that period alone. Mind you, she has not worked for over 16 years but she does not remember that. Quite often she will ask me when she is supposed to go to work. I patiently tell her she has not worked for some time that she is now retired. She always gets a puzzled look about that condition but she accepts it, usually with an amazed look. There have been times when she has asked me about her work ten, fifteen times in a two-minute span.

Moderate cognitive decline Symptomatic of Stage Two

(Mild or early-stage Alzheimer's disease shows cognitive decline is still part of stage two but overlapping with stage one and three)

At this point, a careful medical interview should be able to detect clear-cut symptoms in several areas. This is generally true. I know when we took mom to the Neurologist he recognized her dementia right away and after the brain scan made a determination of her condition, but he did not call it Alzheimer's.

You will notice the symptoms overlap through the stages thus making the determination of the exact stage of development nearly impossible. Sometimes your patient will be in one stage and then suddenly avert to another one. It is impossible to tell from symptoms exactly where your patient's development of progression is and you will not know for sure until they become incapable of caring for themselves and then you might think stage two or possibly stage three.

Usually in stage five or six they can no longer help themselves. Most of the time I have to dress mom, shower her, feed her and yes, there are occasions where her toilet participation is left up to me. The problem is since the symptoms overlap, I too have difficulty identifying the stage development.

Forgetfulness of recent events.

This is a common condition of the disease and as mentioned before, mom's short-term memory is completely gone. I noticed an inability on her part to recall a breakfast meal after a period of one or two minutes. That symptom actually gets worse with time and you will notice your patient will often have difficulty understanding how to swallow. Your patient might forget the purpose of a fork or knife and they will sometimes pick up a fried egg with their fingers and try to spread jelly or butter on it. They might do this in stage two but it is usually stage three or four when these symptoms show up.

Another thing you might notice is your patient might show an inability to understand your statements, that is, they will say yes to your questions and not have a clue what you are talking about, like the egg instance. When you tell your patient that she has an egg in her hand or his hand he or she might answer with a yes but have no idea what it is they have in their hand. This is very common in stage two and develops into a worse condition in stage three.

Spatial Concepts Disappear

Impaired ability to perform simple mental arithmetic

The doctor gave mom a simple test of counting backwards by 7 from 100 and she could not do it. I discovered that I am not very good at that particular task either and I have never been able to recite the alphabet backwards.

We discovered mom could no longer do simple arithmetic. She could no longer solve simple problems. Complex tasks such as washing dishes were no longer part of her daily routine. She still, every now and then will attempt dishwashing but I always have to do them over. She will take a clean towel and wipe water from the floor and then put the towel back on the counter top.

Alzheimer patients simply do not understand that part of hygiene nor do they understand the need for cleanliness. I have to remind mom to wash her hands after toileting and the concept of flushing the toilet leaves sometime during stage two or early three. Your patient will do neither, wash their hands or flush the toilet.

You might find your patient with their feces on their hands or fingers because they no longer understand what it is. If you find yourself queasy under those circumstances you might want to bring in a day nurse to assist you in those tasks. At first, I had some difficulty with some of the things mom did but I am now used to most of her surprises.

Complexity tasking disappears sometime during stage two and or early three

It becomes increasingly difficult for patients to perform complex tasks, such as planning dinner for guests, paying bills or managing finances. The patient becomes frustrated and irritated when they cannot accomplish these simple things because they know somehow they used to do them but now, for some reason they can no longer remember how those things are done.

It has to be very frustrating for an individual when he or she no longer functions properly. My mother-in-law was a very capable woman before this disease took control of her and now she barely functions. The sad part is she will not recover but only get worse. When your patient can no longer accomplish the simple you will discover they can no longer accomplish anything at all.

The Patient's personal history becomes vague.

This is something that really creates difficulties with mom. As her disease progresses, her memory becomes worse; remembering individuals like her husband of more than fifty years seems more like a dream to her, a vague group of pictures that she can no longer remember as a daily routine. She becomes distraught over her loss of memory and in turn she cries, even sobs; she gets irritated at herself for not remembering important things and the distressing part is she knows she should remember but she can't. When she gets that way, she is very difficult to work with. She is not mad at me but at herself.

I often sit with her talking to her about the past and those important people in her dream world. Sometimes she remembers and sometimes she does not, but it never hurts to go over their memories. It never hurts to hold them close and tell them you love them. Your patient might well be your mother or your father. Sometimes they are your husband or wife and I say, give them all the comfort and love you can muster even during the difficult times.

I have watched her go through the stages and there was a time when she would go to the fireplace

mantle and see the picture of her deceased husband and cry for the loss. She did that for a long time, perhaps two years but she no longer recognizes the picture on the mantle and she no longer cries when she sees it. The mantle is gone from her daily routine. Even I am gone from her daily routine. Mom now looks at me with a curious gaze like she wants to question who I am but I usually tell her who I am before she questions. I can see the curious look in her eyes as if she should know me but cannot remember.

Night Time Anxiety

It is important to note that most Alzheimer patients have difficulty sleeping at night. If you leave a light on in their bathroom or their bedroom they will, upon waking, think it daytime. If your patient believes it is daytime, you will have considerable difficulty convincing him or her it is still night. As I mentioned above mom will emerge from her bedroom at 11:00 PM or Midnight fully dressed, purse in hand and ready to go. She has absolutely no idea where she is going but I have on many occasions spent hours convincing her she is already at home and it is still the middle of the night.

Believe me; it is extremely difficult when she gets out of bed ten or fifteen times. Usually, it takes the better part of the night to get her back to bed and by that time I am exhausted. If you have a bad heart or any ailment that requires you get a good night's rest, then taking care of an Alzheimer's patient might not be your best choice.

The responsibility of the caregiver goes far beyond the norm and from my readings, most people cannot cope with the responsibility; they simply burn out after a couple of years. There are many organizations out there that will assist you if the

caregiver responsibilities become more than you can bear.

While I mention organizations willing to help, they are only willing if you have the money. Most states have no programs worth considering and Medicare does not cover any of the costs, only the medicines and I believe that coverage is about 80%. I am told Medicaid will help but they are quite stringent about their support and demanding with their regulations. If you live in Florida, you will get no help from Medicaid until your patient is completely incapacitated and then they will not help until you exhaust all their savings. In other words, if your patient has any money at all, Medicaid will not help until they are completely broke.

If your personal income is about average then taking care of your Alzheimer patient will be most difficult financially. Nearly all available care is cost prohibitive. I only say this because any help you seek will be costly. We will have a young person come in for a few hours a week and it costs about $100.00 a week for her services. Her services are required so I can go to the store and do the various needed errands.

Medicare does not cover any of those costs related to Alzheimer's unless your patient is in their last stage of the disease and unable to respond to any stimuli. When I say respond I mean your patient must be bed ridden and in need of a feeding tube; otherwise, Medicare will not help with a Hospice. Even in the final stage, you will have to get a doctor to sign off on your patient's condition or Hospice will have no authority to offer treatment. In Florida there are very few facilities capable of offering decent services for the Alzheimer patient so, if you live in that state you will have to shop around.

Chapter Seven

Stage Three

Becoming moody or withdrawn, especially in socially or mentally challenging situations.

Stage Three usually brings moderately severe cognitive decline

The caregiver will notice gaps in memory and thinking; individuals begin needing help with day-to-day activities. At this stage, those with Alzheimer's may be unable to recall their own address or telephone number or the high school or college from which they graduated. This particular symptom mom experienced for over a year before we thought of her entering Stage Three. You will find that symptoms quite often overlap according to the cognitive powers of your patient.

Alzheimer patients become confused about where they are or what day it is and they will not understand morning, noon or night. They might inform you they are hungry even after they finish breakfast. My mom will ask about breakfast right after she finishes eating it. Her overall ability to enjoin in the family discussions is completely gone and that ability diminishes beginning Stage Two or at the near end of Stage One.

Your patient might require assistance dressing or figuring out what he or she should wear for the day. An individual suffering from Alzheimer's might put their underwear on their head or put on two, even three pairs of pants. I have seen mom with two bras, one on

the front and one in back. I have watched her put blouses on upside down, backwards and on her legs because the concept of clothes is gone. Yet, she might remember on any given Monday significant details about her family and require no assistance eating or using the toilet. On the other hand, she might not be able on Tuesday to get out of bed and anything to do with eating or toiletries will be completely foreign to her. I have watched her attempt putting her feet into her purse thinking it was her shoe. Yes, I have cried a lot over this disease and I am not done crying.

Your patient might become more combative or more pliable depending upon how their life went but don't ever get complacent about your patient's condition; they can do an about face in less than a second. You will notice at the end of stage three your patient will become more distant and will no longer recognize you or any of the household members. Your patient will be more reticent and less enjoining. They might disqualify themselves completely from all family members and associations. It is not something they desire, it is something they will do because they no longer understand conversation and they no longer recognize family.

Chapter Eight
Stage Four
Stage Four generally brings about considerably severe cognitive decline

During this stage your patient might suffer personality changes. You might experience the Jekyl/Hyde personalities on and off during the day. It will be a curious thing to witness because the sweet individual you always knew might well begin using language that would make a truck driver blush. The patient's memory continues to worsen, personality changes may take place and individuals need extensive help with daily activities. At this stage, individuals may lose awareness of recent experiences as well as of their surroundings. They will probably forget the names of close relatives, brothers, and sisters, even their own children.

Forgetting family members can begin in stage three and get progressively worse. Mom often forgets my name and sometimes refers to me as the strange man in the house. When I tell her I'm her son-in-law she just stares at me with a blank stare. I can tell when she does that she is trying to remember but nothing comes to mind.

Sometime last year we moved to a new home but we still own our old home. Mom has never figured out the layout of the new home and when we visit the other place she heads straight for her old bedroom. However, now that she is in stage four, her old bedroom is no longer a memory. When we visit the old house she sits in the car and waits; she no longer recognizes the place, though we lived there for five years.

We have lived in the new house for one year now and she still cannot remember the location of either her bathroom or her bedroom.

Our kitchen is centralized so it has three entrances; they constantly confuse her; she cannot grasp the concept that one can enter the kitchen from the bedroom hallway, the dining room or the living room.

Alzheimer patients are easily confused so it is best to offer them a simple environment. Even in simplicity they still get confused and in mom's case, she will walk around the kitchen, find an exit and come around the circle and enter the kitchen again. She will do that three or four times until either my wife or I steer her in the right direction.

Stage Four patients show certain signs of deterioration when it comes to dressing themselves. They may and often do put their clothes on wrong as mentioned before. They may not be able to put their shoes on the correct feet and if they have shoes that must be tied, it is a chore just watching them; tying shoes is impossible for most patients entering Stage Four of this disease. I suggest you change your patient's shoes to something simple like a pull on sandal with an elastic strap that goes around the back of the heel.

Mom could still tie her shoes a month ago but I changed her shoes to a pull on sandals anyway because she had too much difficulty bending over. You might find your patient struggling to do simple tasks such as bending over or just lifting their feet off the floor. A common symptom of this stage is your patient's inability to bend over, stand up quickly, negotiate corners while walking, shortness of breath, and lack of understanding food items.

Stage Four patients will not remember how to lift their feet from the floor. They will no longer respond to commands such as, "Pick up your left foot so I can put on this sock..." Those verbalizations are useless. It is better to get down on the floor and pick the foot up and then put on the sock and shoe.

Stage Four patients, for the most part, cannot dress themselves or take a shower. They no longer comprehend verbal directions. They might answer with a 'Yes' but they will not respond to your voice. They will not understand the concept of personal hygiene and that might start in stage two. If they have dentures, you must clean them. If they still have their own teeth, you must brush them. If they use the toilet, you will probably have to clean it after they finish and they will no longer remember to flush after use.

Fourth Stage Alzheimer patients will have to wear some sort of personal protection to guard against accidental urination or defecation. Quite often they will walk down a hallway dropping their wares as they go. You will quickly adjust to them wearing some sort of protection. If you do not put these protective clothing on your patient you will be doing a great deal of sanitizing.

My mother-in-law can no longer effectively dress herself, nor can she take a shower by herself. She will, quite often, put her nightgown on over her pants. The inability to dress oneself usually comes during the Fourth Stage but with mom I seen the beginnings of the symptom in stage two.

Mom has experienced major difficulties and changes in her sleep patterns. As I mentioned before, if the lights are left on Alzheimer patients might think it is daytime while it is still midnight. They will be restless and sometimes argumentative at night. They will sleep during the day and keep you up all night. You will also

discover that your patient will not be able to control their bladder or their bowel movements. You will do a great deal of floor cleaning and bathroom cleaning at the end of stage three and through stage four.

There is no doubt the caregiver must have a world of patience. If you do not have a lot of patience, you will not be able to handle the job of caregiver. Mom frequently forgets who I am and often refuses to listen to me. She will think I am a criminal trying to hurt her. The interesting thing about her delusions is they might only last a few minutes, but during those few minutes she can be quite challenging. You might notice your patient wringing his or her hands and tearing tissues into small pieces. Mom takes the tissues and the napkins from the restaurants and puts them in her bra. Sometimes at night when I get her ready for bed she will have as many as twenty tissues stuffed in her bra.

Your Patient Might Become A Kleptomaniac

Kleptomania is another interesting symptom of this disease. Your patient might begin hoarding different memorabilia, things from the past. The patient will pick up pictures or other items that identify their existence and they will hide them.

I do coffee cup designs and I made a cup that said, 'Ron's Cup of Music.' Mom really liked the cup and she would take it into her bedroom and hide it in her dresser or under the bed. Sometimes she will even put it under her pillow. This behavior pattern is quite common and understandable. In order to keep my cup in the kitchen, I made her a cup that said about the same message. Now she hides them both.

The one thing you can never do is admonish them for their little idiosyncrasies; they do not remember doing anything the following day. I

discovered when I found my cup in her bedroom that any suggestion that she was a Klepto, even in jest, seemed to upset her, so I quit talking about it and just returned the cup to its rightful place.

Alzheimer Patients Can Become Delusional

You might find your patient experiences major personality and behavioral changes. Sometimes mom will believe me a complete stranger and she will think I have entered the house to hurt or injure her. She becomes suspicious. She has on occasion believed me an imposter. If your patient goes through this type of delusion do not become alarmed. Fifteen minutes later they will not remember the incident and everything will be fine. Mind you, mom carried on for a full day about me being an imposter and she was positive I did something to Ron.

There was no amount of talking that convinced her of anything different. I finally had to admit to myself that I was an intruder. She did not have a phone so she could not call the police. She did threaten.

Chapter Nine

Patients Tend to wander
or
become lost

Stage Five of this disease reveals very severe cognitive decline

It is never a good idea to leave your patient unattended or alone.

In Stage Five your patient will show very serious signs of deterioration. They will become quite often unresponsive to your voice. They will often times stare into space without regard to you or anyone in the home. They will sometimes sit in one spot for hours without communicating.

Their communications might be in the form of saying things like “yes, uh, uh” or something like just sitting and rocking back and forth. They will often times try to cut their toast or pick up a fried egg. They will not understand the utensils like the fork or the knife. Their ability to communicate will be narrowed down to one or two words. The symptoms might last all day or even more than one day. All of the sudden they will be responsive again and seemingly back to stage three normalcy.

Don’t be fooled by this sudden turnaround in symptoms. Alzheimer patients will go through different stages of the disease and they might experience stage six during their stage five experience. You will

unexpectedly see stage three or stage two symptoms and wonder what is going on. These transfers back through stages are part of the disease. When your patient gets to stage five they will have fewer moments of coherency and they will experience fewer moments of cognition. Their cognitive powers will be limited to fewer words and sometimes no words at all.

You might see your patient walking around the house picking things up and examining them with a strange curiosity. I have questioned mom when I see her do this and she has told me that she is looking at things, beautiful things that she hadn't seen before. Mom also, during stages four and five, would go to pictures on the fireplace mantle and pick them up. After a moment she would cry. I would ask her why she was crying and she would say things like. My husband is no longer here or my brother was such a wonderful man.

As late stage four and early five take hold, those trips to the mantle and around the house become fewer. The changes are subtle but if you watch closely, you will begin to notice the differences.

Memory is a marvelous thing and a dreaded thing to lose. My mother-in-law is fully aware that she is losing her memory and fully aware that it is the result of Alzheimer's. Occasionally she will ask if there is anything that can be done and I will tell her, 'there is no cure.' I usually say something directive about old age and how we lose our memories. Sometimes I tell her I suffer from the same memory loss that it is a part of growing old. Sometimes my answers will make her sad and other times she will respond with answers like, "Oh well, I'm too old and useless to be around anyway." When she gets in one of those moods I find the best thing is a long hug and a quiet kiss followed by a statement like, "We love you very much."

There are times when mom will be in one of her Mr. Hyde moods, as I call them. Usually, a hug or a kiss will bring her out of those moods. People who are generally sweet do not like being anything but sweet. When they are in a bitter mood, they do not really like that mood.

Mom will always stop and talk to people in the grocery store, especially if they say something to her to initiate the conversation. She loves little children and will always touch them and tell the parents how precious their children are. This is really just another manifestation of the disease. As the caregiver, you will see all these symptoms or perhaps most of them in different forms.

Chapter Ten

Stage Six Alzheimer's

Your Patient will suffer from nearly a complete loss of Cognition

Stage Six, sometimes confused with stage seven is a devastating turn of events. Your patient will not remember how to control bowel movements or urination. They will often times forget how to eat and how to handle their eating utensils. These symptoms will start in Stage Five and then continue to worsen through Stage Six. You will find yourself feeding your patient but even that will come to an end. They will forget how to swallow and when that happens, they usually no longer respond to you or anyone else. The disease simply shuts down the brain until there is nothing left of the person you loved.

This disease is the worst experience I have witnessed in my entire 76 years. I have been in combat situations, barroom fights, and every kind of weird mission the government could throw at me but I never experienced anything like Alzheimer's. That once beautiful person I knew and loved is completely gone and she will not return.

At this point in the development of this disease it might be best for you and the family to place your loved one in a care facility. At a care facility they will be made comfortable and Hospice can come in and take care of their personal needs. Some of us are too stubborn to give up and we take the duties on to ourselves. That would be an admirable gesture on your part but if you have other family or a career you must also consider your responsibilities to those situations.

My wife and I have had considerable discussions about mom and about responsibility. Since I am older than my wife, she worries that taking care of her mother might be too difficult for me. She also does not want to give up our years together. I do not believe her selfish but realistic. I just came out of the hospital from a bout with blood pressure, 210/103, pretty high considering my blood pressure usually runs 120/72. I believe my wife has a good point about the stress level of taking care of her mother.

I am certain the high blood pressure was the result of a new medicine but I cannot rule out the possibility of just plain stress. I did however notice the high blood pressure went away after I quit taking the new medicine and I have been out of the hospital for over a week now and my blood pressure has returned to normal. That does not mean it won't suddenly skyrocket again, so I am watching it closely.

In the meantime a decision had to be made as to mom's care. We did decide on a home that deals specifically with Alzheimer patients. The most difficult thing for me is the letting go. That sudden realization that mom will never return is the worst part of this disease.

I suggest that you as a caregiver must be ready to make those decisions and you can't let your personal feelings get in the way. I have nothing but great admiration for those of you who refuse to give up but sometimes it is best for you and your patient to know when to let go.

Chapter Eleven

Stage Seven
The Final Stage

This stage of the disease is the one that actually breaks your heart. Your patient will deteriorate to a near comatose state and they could remain in that state for as much as a year, depending upon you as the caregiver. If you have the patient's POA then it will be up to you to make the final decisions.

When your patient enters the final stage of this disease, he or she will lose the ability to respond to their environment, to carry on a conversation and, eventually, to control movement. They may still say words or phrases but they will be few and often incoherent.

At this stage, individuals need help with much of their daily personal care, including eating or using the toilet. They may also lose the ability to smile, sit without support or hold their heads up. Reflexes become abnormal. Muscles grow rigid and their swallowing impaired. This heart breaking disease will make the most macho man cry and if the patient is your mother or father, you will die a little with them. I had a minister; while I was in the hospital, tell me it was the longest funeral one could ever attend—he was right.

Your patient's mood swings will probably be unmanageable and his or her demands will be unreasonable. They might be unresponsive, moody, friendly, irrational and hateful. When lucid your patient might just want to give up and die. You will find yourself perplexed at the behavior, yet it is part of

the disease. You must recognize it is the final stage and your loved one is gone.

We placed mom in the home on December 10th 2012. Around January 1st she fell and broke her hip and suffered a hemorrhage in frontal lobe of her brain. The on call doctor got her to a local hospital and they transferred her to another hospital where she could get better care. Her living will forbid any treatment like feeding tubes or hip surgery and actually the doctors did not feel secure doing any kind of surgery because of the hemorrhage. As a result of her injuries, mom died on January 14th, 2013.

So, what are some of the secrets I have learned as a caregiver that will help you deal with your patient?

First: you need the patience of Job in order to keep your cool. If you become angry or frustrated, you will quickly learn that those tactics do not work. People with Alzheimer's are still very sensitive to moods and they respond to your negativism with irrational behavior.

Second: If you show signs of anger you might get a response you do not like. Alzheimer patients sometimes give the impression of being possessed. If you believe in demons, you might just meet one if you bring your patient to anger. You might also find if you are attempting to restrain them that they are very strong and completely determined to do their own will.

Your best possible approach to bad behavior is offer them all the love you can and patience is the best virtue. Never try to force your patient to do anything they do not want to do. It is better to wait for their mood to change than to attempt any force about the issue. Your patience is the key to successful caregiving.

Third: Be respectful of their dignity and mindful of their needs. I found taking care of mom a blessing, not a curse. I loved her as any son could love his mother, maybe more.

I am certain if you understand this disease as a caregiver you will offer your loved one an environment conducive to their needs. Just be patient and calm, full of love and caring. Follow those principles; be loving, kind and mindful. Simple steps offer simple solutions. Consider it a blessing taking care of a loved one suffering from a complex disease.

Ron

Conclusion

I hope this synopsis of the disease called Alzheimer's has been of some assistance to you as a caregiver.

Yes, I cry for her and I cry for those of us who have to let go but I convince myself it is for the best.

May God love you and protect you in your challenge with this disease.

Ron

Credits:

Mayo Clinic
Ask.com
AlzResourceCenter.com

www.ingramcontent.com/pod-product-compliance
Ingram Content Group UK Ltd.
Pitfield, Milton Keynes, MK11 3LW, UK
UKHW041924190726
13854UKWH00003B/1439